Snapdragons
Stage 1+
Shirley Bickler

Teaching Notes

Contents

Introduction

The *Snapdragons* series is a rich mix of different kinds of stories presented as picture books with expertly written text carefully levelled to provide reading practice at each stage in Key Stage 1.

This set of six books at Stage 1+ concentrates on developing the very early reading skills that children need to become competent readers. It includes six very simple stories told in patterned language with a predictable structure. These stories introduce children to early key words as well as useful vocabulary relating to the different contexts.

The stories at Stage 1+ are all based in familiar settings: the home, the high street, the park, the shops, the farm and forms of transport. They reflect everyday life and the readers will quickly identify with the family members and pets, and recognise their experiences.

These simple books at Stage 1+ allow children to learn how stories work, and the order and direction in which they are read. Children are encouraged to look at the illustrations for visual cues to the words in the text, and to find out what is happening in the story. The picture book presentation will also encourage children to tell the story in their own words and develop their oral skills.

How to introduce the books

Before reading the story for guided or independent reading, always read the title and talk about the picture on the cover.

Go through the book together, looking at the pictures and talking about them. If there are context words (listed in the chart on page 4) that are new or unfamiliar, point them out and read them with the children. Read the story to the children, encouraging confident children to join in with you.

This booklet provides prompts and suggestions for using the books in groups and for guided, group and independent activities, matched to text, sentence and word level objectives. There are also separate Guided Reading Cards available for six titles at each stage.

Suggestions are also provided for speaking and listening activities, writing activities, and cross-curricular links. You can use these suggestions to follow on from your reading or at another time.

Reading notes are also provided in each book. They can be found on the inside front and back covers of each book. These suggest friendly prompts and activities for parents or carers reading with their children at home.

Reading skills

Stage 1+ is essential for:

- introducing the main characters
- encouraging children to talk about themselves and their experiences in relation to the stories
- developing a positive attitude towards reading
- teaching initial book-handling skills
- developing listening skills
- introducing the first key words
- developing an understanding of the story.

Stage 1+ develops:

- an understanding of text and the way it behaves
- book-handling skills
- phonological awareness, i.e. the awareness that letters are symbols for sounds.

Vocabulary chart

Stage 1+		
My Dad	Year R High frequency words	on is a big my dad
	Context words	trousers boots jacket hat gloves fire engine
Going Up and Down	Year R High frequency words	I am going look at me up and
	Context words	round dizzy
Where is Baby?	Year R High frequency words	I can see on the is
	Context words	baby jam floor door coat boat bear stairs cat asleep mat
Breakfast	Year R High frequency words	I went to see the said for like
	Context words	breakfast you cows goats horse hens
My Dog Needs a Bone	Year R High frequency words	I my dog a like big this
	Context words	needs dish red collar long lead bed
Hello Grandma!	Year R High frequency words	we got in a went on the
	Context words	car train bus plane dinner tea sleep Grandma hello Nanni-ji

Curriculum coverage chart

Stage 1	Speaking and listening	Reading	Writing
My Dad			
NLS/NC	1d, 1e, 8a	T7, S3, W6, W9, W14	T12, T13, T14
Scotland	working towards Level A	working towards Level A	working towards Level A
N. Ireland	Activities: a, b, c Outcomes: b, c, d, e	Activities: c, e Outcomes: b, c, e, f	Outcomes: a, b, c
Wales	Range: 1, 3, 5 Skills: 2, 3	Range: 1, 2, 4, 5, 6 Skills: 1, 2	Range: 1, 2, 3, 4, 6, 7 Skills: 1, 2, 3, 4, 5
Going Up and Down			
NLS/NC	1b, 1d, 1e	T7, S3, W7	T12, T13, T14
Scotland	working towards Level A	working towards Level A	working towards Level A
N. Ireland	Activities: b, e Outcomes: b, c, d, e	Activities: a, b, c, e Outcomes: b, c, d	Outcomes: a, b, c
Wales	Range: 1, 3 Skills: 1, 2, 3	Range:1, 2, 4, 5, 6 Skills: 1, 2	Range: 1, 2, 3, 4, 6, 7 Skills: 1, 2, 3, 4, 5
Where is Baby?			
NLS/NC	2c, 3a, 4b	T7, T8, S4, W1, W4	T12
Scotland	working towards Level A	working towards Level A	working towards Level A
N. Ireland	Activities: a, b Outcomes: a, c, d	Activities: a, b, e Outcomes: b, c, d	Outcomes: b, c
Wales	Range: 1, 2, 3 Skills: 2, 5, 6	Range: 1, 2, 4, 5, 6 Skills: 1, 2	Range: 1, 2, 3, 4, 6, 7 Skills: 1, 2, 5
Breakfast			
NLS/NC	3a, 4a, 4b	T8, S3, W2	T11
Scotland	working towards Level A	working towards Level A	working towards Level A
N. Ireland	Activities: b, c, g Outcomes: b, c, d, e	Activities: a, b Outcomes: b, c, d, f	Outcomes: b, c, f
Wales	Range: 1, 2, 3, 5 Skills: 1, 2, 3, 4	Range:1, 2, 4, 5, 6 Skills: 1, 2	Range: 1, 2, 3, 4, 6, 7 Skills: 1, 2, 3
My Dog Needs a Bone			
NLS/NC	2a, 2c, 3a	T6, S1, W4	T14, T15
Scotland	working towards Level A	working towards Level A	working towards Level A
N. Ireland	Activities: a, b, f, g Outcomes: a, b, c, d, e	Activities: b, c, e Outcomes: b, c, d, e	Outcomes: a, b, c
Wales	Range: 1, 2, 3 Skills: 1, 2, 3, 4	Range: 1, 2, 4, 5, 6 Skills: 1, 2	Range: 1, 2, 3, 4, 6, 7 Skills: 1, 2, 3, 4
Hello Grandma!			
NLS/NC	1e, 4a, 4c	T8, T11, S1, W4	T12, T14
Scotland	working towards Level A	working towards Level A	working towards Level A
N. Ireland	Activities: b, c, e, g Outcomes: a, b, d	Activities: b, c Outcomes: b, c, d, f	Outcomes: b, c
Wales	Range: 1, 2, 5, 6 Skills: 1, 2, 3	Range:1, 2, 4, 5, 6 Skills: 1, 2	Range: 1, 2, 3, 4, 6, 7 Skills: 1, 8

My Dad

Reading the story

Introducing the story

- Read the title and look at page 1. Ask the children: *Why do you think Dad put on big boots like these?*
- Look through the illustrations and ask the children if they guessed what Dad's job was.
- Draw attention to the story line on the last page.

During reading

- Praise the children for pointing under each word carefully as they read.
- Praise children for using the illustrations to support their reading of interest words.
- Encourage the children to read the words in speech bubbles expressively.

Observing Check that the children:

- point to the words as they read, understanding the significance of the spaces between the words
- make use of the illustrations to help read interest words
- check their reading of the last page makes sense.

Group and independent reading activities

Text level work

Range familiar setting/predictable structure/patterned language

Objective To use knowledge of familiar texts to re-enact or re-tell to others, recounting the main points in correct sequence (T7).

You will need big trousers, boots, a big jacket, a hat (helmet), gloves, and chairs to represent the fire engine.

- Ask the children to take turns to be Dad and the Reader.

- The Reader reads the text, Dad puts on appropriate garments, and the rest of the children sit on the chairs and chant, *"Hurry up!"*
- The Reader reads the last page, Dad jumps on the fire engine (a chair) and everyone shouts, *"NEE NAW!"*

Observing Does each child manage his or her role appropriately?

Sentence level work

Objective That words are ordered from left to right and need to be read that way to make sense (S3).

You will need the following word cards:
Dad, put, on, a, big, trousers, boots, jacket, hat, gloves

- Ask the children to put the words in order to make sentences from the story.
- Re-read each sentence, pointing carefully under each word.

Observing Do the children check their sentences by re-reading? Can the children use the initial letter of the interest words to help them read unfamiliar vocabulary?

Word level work

Objectives To read on sight YR high frequency words (W6); To recognise the critical features of words (W9); To write letters using the correct sequence of movements (W14).

- Ask children to locate "Dad", "big", "on" or "up" in the text on each page of the book (choose a new word for the group).
- Demonstrate how to write the word using the correct sequence of movements for each letter.
- Ask the children to write and re-write the word across their whiteboards, leaving spaces between each attempt.

Observing Can the children write without checking the text? Are they using correct letter formations? Do they remember to leave a space between each word?

Speaking and listening activities

Objectives Focus on the main point(s) (1d); include relevant detail (1e); telling stories, real and imagined (8a).

- Look through the book and talk about what Dad did in sequence (e.g. *First Dad put on... Then he put on... Next he... The last thing he ...*).
- Mime an activity for the children, e.g. cleaning your teeth. Repeat the actions and ask the children to put them into words in the right sequence.
- Ask a child to mime an activity, e.g. making a sandwich, and ask another child to put the sequence into words.
- Use puppets to tell a familiar story and describe the sequence of events.

Cross-curricular link
Citizenship: valuing people in the community

Writing

Objectives To write captions for pictures and drawings (T12); To think about and discuss what they intend to write, ahead of writing it (T13); To use experience of stories as a basis for independent writing (T14).

- Ask: *What would you like to be when you grow up?*
- Discuss what kind of clothing they think they will need for their job.
- Encourage them to draw or paint a picture of themselves dressed for their job.
- Using the text as a model, ask them to write in the third person, e.g. "Tom put on overalls/a black suit/white coat." If necessary help them write any unfamiliar words.

Going Up and Down

Reading the story

Introducing the story

- Read the title with the children. Ask the children: *How are the words "Up" and "Down" written? Why?*
- Look through the illustrations, asking: *Where is the child is going?*
- On page 11, ask: *How might the child feel after going round and round?* Look at page 12 to see if they were right.

During reading

- Praise the children for looking at the illustrations to help them work out the words.
- Encourage the children to read the speech bubbles with expression.
- Praise children who track the text accurately, pointing to each word as they read.

Observing Check that the children:

- point to each word as they read
- change their expression for reading the main text and speech bubbles.

Group and independent reading activities

Text level work

Range familiar setting/predictable structure/patterned language

Objective To use knowledge of familiar texts to re-enact or re-tell to others (T7).

You will need cards with the following sentences from the book:
I am going up.   I am going in.   I am going out.
I am going down.   I am going up and down.
I am going round and round.

- Ask the children to take turns to read a card and mime the action.

- Suggest they mime different situations, e.g. going up a steep hill; round on a bicycle.
- Ask the children to take turns to mime while others find the card that matches the action.

Observing Can they think of other situations in which they go up, down or round and round, and so on?

Sentence level work

Objective To know that words are ordered left to right and need to be read that way to make sense (S3).

You will need the following unfinished sentence strip and word cards for each child:
I am going…
down, up, in, out, round, and, round

- Turn to page 3. Cover the text at the bottom of the page.
- Ask the children to select the appropriate word card and complete the sentence: "I am going down".
- Ask the children to re-read their sentence and check it with the text on the page. Repeat for other pages.

Observing How does each child select the missing word/words? Does each child re-read spontaneously? Are they able to check accurately?

Word level work

Objective To read on sight the words from texts of appropriate difficulty (W7).

You will need two sets of cards with the following words:
I, am, going, look, at, me, and, up

- Place the cards face down randomly. Children take turns to turn up two cards. If they match, the cards must be read correctly before the child keeps them. If not, the cards are turned face down again, and another child has a turn.
- The child with the most pairs wins.

Observing Can the children read high frequency words with confidence? Can they follow the rules of the game?

Speaking and listening activities

Objectives Choose words with precision (1b); focus on the main point(s) (1d); include relevant detail (1e).

- Tell the children that they are going to change the story. They are going to give the child a name.
- Start to re-tell the story, e.g. *One Saturday afternoon Chen went to the park*. Ask the children to take turns to continue, e.g. *Chen went on the slide. He said, "I am going up."*

Observing Are the children able to adapt their language? Can they add relevant details to the story?

◀▶ **Cross-curricular link**
Numeracy: understanding properties of position and movement

Writing

Objectives To write sentences to match pictures (T12); To think about and discuss what they intend to write, ahead of writing it (T13); To use experience of stories as a basis for independent writing (T14).

You will need blank paper and pencils or crayons, or photos of each child in the playground.

- Ask each child to draw a picture of him or her in the playground, going up, down, in, out or round something. Alternatively, mount the photos on paper.
- Help the children write a two-sentence caption, e.g. "I am going down. Look at me."
- Help them to write their story under the picture.
- Mount the pictures, and print the text in large print underneath so that others can read it.

Where is Baby?

Reading the story

Introducing the story

- Look at the cover together. Ask the children: *Can you spot something interesting in the title?* (A question mark.) Help them to read the title.
- As they look through the illustrations, tell them that the boy can see clues to help him find the baby.
- On the last page, ask: *What is baby doing?*

During reading

- Draw attention to the question mark on page 2 and in the speech bubbles.
- Praise careful pointing at words as they read.
- Praise children for using illustrations and initial letters to read interest words.
- Praise children for using the meaning and print to guess words, e.g. "steps" for "stairs". Praise and prompt for a closer look through the word.

Observing Check that the children:

- read in a rhythmic manner, emphasising rhyming words
- retain accurate pointing
- read the text on the last page carefully.

Group and independent reading activities

Text level work

Range familiar setting/predictable structure/patterned language/rhyme

Objectives To use the knowledge of familiar texts to re-enact or re-tell to others (T7); To locate and read significant parts of the text (T8).

- Discuss the importance of the punctuation in the title.

- Model a questioning tone and ask children to locate and read questions throughout the text.
- Discuss the role of the boy as a detective . Ask: *Is he puzzled, annoyed or excited?* Model the different tones of voice.
- Pick an emotion and ask a child to read lines of text with matching expression.
- Re-read the story together with expression.

Observing Do the children retain one-to-one correspondence as they read expressively? Do they read with expression throughout?

Sentence level work

Objective To use a capital letter for the start of own name (S4).

- Ask the children to locate capital letters in the title and speech bubbles. Discuss the use of capital letters at the beginning of sentences and names.
- With the children, scribe a new version of the story using one of the children's names , e.g. "Where is Samira?"; "I can see paint on the..."; "I can see paint on the...". Emphasise the importance of the capital letter at the beginning of the child's name. (Ignore the rhyming aspect of the text for this activity.)

Observing Check that each child can use the term "capital letter" and understands that there are two forms of each letter.

Word level work

Objectives To understand and be able to rhyme and extend these patterns through extending these patterns by analogy (W1); To link sound and spelling patterns (W4).

- Read the rhyming couplets, asking the children to supply the last word. Ask them to make up a third and fourth line, using nonsense words if necessary.
- Scribe the rhyming words and discuss the link between the sound and the spelling.

Observing Check that the children enjoy this activity. Can they hear the rhymes and also make links with the initial letters?

Speaking and listening activities

Objectives Make relevant comments (2c); take turns in speaking (3a); create and sustain roles individually and when working with others (4b).

You will need a box and some puppets, preferably modelled on animals as well as people.

- Ask one child to select a puppet and hide it in the box.
- As the child gradually reveals the puppet, the other children take turns to describe what they can see, e.g. "I can see a finger." "I can see a sleeve."
- The first child to guess the identity of the puppet has the next turn.

Cross-curricular link
Music: using voices expressively by speaking chants and rhymes

Writing

Objective To experiment with writing and recognise how their own version matches and differs from conventional version (T12).

You will need a selection of pictures of common objects.

- Explain to the children that they are going to solve some riddles. Select a picture of an object and scribe a description on the whiteboard:
  I can see a lid.
  I can see a handle.
  I can see a spout.
  What is it?
- Ask the children to take turns to select a picture and make up their own riddle. Act as a scribe for them.
- Ask them to choose another object and write their own riddles.

Breakfast

Reading the story

Introducing the story

- Read the title with the children. Tell them that in this book, a boy shows us how he gave lots of farm animals their breakfast.
- Talk through the illustrations, helping the children understand that this story is in the form of a report.
- On page 12, Ask: *Who's breakfast would this be?*

During reading

- Direct children to the illustrations to help them decode the interest words. Praise them for noticing the initial letters of these words.
- Praise the children for careful, accurate tracking.
- Praise children for reading the direct speech with expression.

Observing Check that the children:

- rerun if necessary to achieve one-to-one tracking
- use a combination of illustrations and initial letters to read interest words
- read at a reasonable speed and with expression.

Group and independent reading activities

Text level work

Range familiar setting/predictable structure/patterned language

Objective To locate and read significant parts of the text (T8).

- Ask the children to turn to page 5. Point out the speech marks, and ask them to put their forefingers on both sets. Say: *These marks tell us to change our voices when we read this part.*
- Remind them that the words inside the marks are what the boy in the story said.
- Go through the book, reading just the speech (on pages 7, 9, 11 and 12).

- Re-read the book together, reading the words inside the speech marks with expression, to sound like talking.

Observing Do the children better understand the purpose of speech marks?

Sentence level work

Objective That words are ordered from left to right and need to be read that way to make sense (S3).

You will need the following unfinished sentence strip and additional word cards:
I went to see…
horses, goats, dogs, rabbits, lambs, ducks

- Ask the children to read the strip of card. Ask: *Do you think that makes sense? What else do you need?*
- Ask a child to choose a word to complete the sentence, and to re-read it.
- Continue in this way, the children taking turns to choose a card.

Observing Check that each child can track, and use structure and text information to complete the sentence.

Word level work

Objective To have knowledge of grapheme/phoneme correspondences through hearing and identifying initial sounds in words (W2).

- Start an unfinished sentence: *I went to see the h…* . Ask: *Which animal did I go and see?*
- Ask the children which animal begins with the letter sound "h".
- Let the children take turns to say a sentence, choosing another animal and initial sound.
- You may wish to ask the children to write the initial letter.

Observing Is each child able to give the appropriate initial letter sound (and write it)?

Speaking and listening activities

Objective Take turns in speaking (3a); use language and emotions to explore and convey situations, characters and emotions (4a); create and sustain roles individually and when working with others (4b).

You will need a container of animal food, such as carrots.

- Choose one child to be a zookeeper. The others take the roles of different zoo animals, each in its own cage.
- Ask the children to act out their own version of the story, adding their own responses, e.g.
  Zookeeper: "Good morning, giraffe. It's breakfast time and I've got some yummy carrots for you."
  Giraffe: "Thank you, Mr Zookeeper. Can I have some hay as well, please?"
- Praise creative dialogue.

◀▶ **Cross-curricular link**
Science: life processes and living things – caring for animals

Writing

Objective To understand how letters are formed and used to spell words; to apply knowledge of letter/sound correspondences in helping the teacher to scribe (T11).

- Ask the children to draw a farm animal.
- Rule lines for each child to write: "I went to see the…". Help the child write the name of the animal he or she has drawn.
- Ask the child to re-read the sentence.
- Print the text so that other children can read it. Bind all the work into a class book.

My Dog Needs a Bone

Reading the story

Introducing the story

- Read the title. Ask the children: *What do you think this story is about?*
- Look through the illustrations with the children, asking what other things the dog needs.
- Draw attention to the speech bubbles and the adjectives on each right-hand page.

During reading

- Re-read the title. Use as an aid to reading page 2 if necessary.
- Praise expressive reading of the speech bubbles.
- When the children are reading "red" (p7) or "long" (p9) suggest that they check the illustrations and sound the first letters. Ask them to re-read the sentence.

Observing Check that the children:

- track the text carefully
- make full use of the illustrations to read the interest words
- read the speech bubbles with expression.

Group and independent reading activities

Text level work

Range familiar setting/predictable structure/patterned language

Objective To re-read frequently a variety of familiar texts (T6).

- Divide the group into pairs. Ask one child to read the main text and the other the speech bubbles.
- Ask the children to close their books. One child in the pair then says, "My dog needs a l…" (lead). The other child must turn to the correct page and read, "I like this long lead."

- That child then says, "My dog needs a b...," (bed) and the other child looks for the right page to read the second sentence.

Observing Is each child able to recall the different objects and provide appropriate initial letters?

Sentence level work

Objective To expect written text to make sense and to check if it does not (S1).

You will need the following unfinished sentence strip and additional word cards:
My dog needs a big ....
sock, ball, pat, hat, hug, truck, mug
If necessary, illustrate the unfamiliar words.

- Place one of the nouns in turn at the end of the sentence.
- Ask the children to read the sentences and judge whether it makes sense.
- Ask the children to make up their own nonsense words for the sentence.

Observing Is each child able to think about the sense and make decisions independently?

Word level work

Objective To link sound and spelling patterns by identifying alliteration in known and new and invented words (W4).

- With the children, read "big bone" (p3) and "long lead" (p9). For each, ask: *Can you hear the initial letter sounds?*
- Ask the children to make up similar phrases for other animals, e.g. big/brown bear, clever/cuddly cat, lonely leopard, sly/silent snake.
- Scribe the children's pairs of words so that they can check them for alliteration.

Observing Are the children able to isolate the letter sounds effectively? Can they check their own suggestions for alliteration?

Speaking and listening activities

Objectives Sustain concentration (2a); make relevant comments (2c); take turns in speaking (3a).

- Ask the children to select a pretend pet and to think about what they would need, e.g. place to live, food to eat, something to play with.
- Encourage the children to say what their pet would need for each category, e.g. "My mouse needs a cage, seeds to eat, a wheel to play on".
- Select a different pet and ask them to guess the animal from things it needs, e.g. "My pet needs a field to live in, grass to eat …".

Cross-curricular link
Science: life processes and living things

Writing

Objectives To use experience of stories as a basis of independent writing (T14); To use writing to communicate in a variety of ways, e.g. lists (T15).

- Using the list in the book as an example, ask the children to write a list of the things they like for lunch (or need for an event or activity).
- Model the sounding out and writing of food, e.g. milk, to(a)st, cof(f)ee.
- Ask them to draw a picture of the food beside each item on the list.
- Mount the lists on a chart headed: "*We like these things for lunch*". Entitle each list with the child's name, e.g. Sharon likes…, Chua likes… .

Hello Grandma!

Reading the story

Introducing the story

- Ask the children to study the cover and predict what the book might be about.
- Identify the girl as the person telling us what happened when the family went to visit Grandma.
- Link the speech-bubble text on page 11 with the title.

During reading

- Prompt the children to look carefully at the text and to check for sense as they read, e.g. on page 2, ask: *What does this word start with*? (got) Does "got" make sense?
- Praise children for looking carefully at the text. On page 8, ask: How did you know that was "dinner"/"tea"?
- Praise children for reading the text in speech bubbles expressively.

Observing Check that the children:

- track the text as they read
- re-read and self-correct using meaning, syntax and print
- respond flexibly to the different sentence structures.

Group and independent reading activities

Text level work

Range familiar setting/predictable structure/patterned language

Objectives To locate and read significant parts of the text (T8); Through shared writing, to apply knowledge of letter/sound correspondences in helping the teacher to scribe (T11).

You will need post-it notes.

- Ask the children to re-read pages 11 and 12, and check they understand the term "speech bubble".

- Ask the children to help write speech bubbles for other parts of the story. Using post-it notes, add speech bubbles, e.g. p2 "Do not forget your bag"; p4 "Hurry up, Dad!"

Observing Are the children able to suggest speech that is relevant to particular situations?

Sentence level work

Objective To expect written text to make sense and to check for sense if it does not (S1).

You will need the following unfinished sentence strips and coloured word cards:
We went on a... We had...
taxi, train, plane, bus, lunch, tea

- Ask the children to read the words on the strips. Ask: *Do they make sense?*
- Ask the children to take turns to select coloured word cards to complete the sentences, and to re-read to check they make sense.

Observing Are the children able to choose appropriate words?

Word level work

Objective To link sound and spelling patterns by using knowledge of rhyme to identify families of rhyming CVC words (W4).

You will need magnetic letters or individual cards with the following letters and vowels:
g, t, h, d, b, s, p a, e, i, o

- Display all the letters. Construct the word "got" and ask the children to sound the phonemes. Change the initial letter to "p", "h", then "d", asking the children to read each new word.
- Change the medial letter to "e" and ask the children to sound out the word and read it. Change the initial letter to read "set", "bet" and "pet".

- Carry out similar changes, starting with "had", "sad", "bad", "pad"; then "sat", "hat", "pat", "bat".

Observing How well does each child blend letter sounds to read new words?

Speaking and listening activities

Objectives Include relevant detail (1e); use language and emotions to explore and convey situations, characters and emotions (4a); comment constructively on drama they have watched or in which they have taken part (4c).

- Ask the children to mime a visit they have made to their grandma, cousin or friend. The rest of the children are going to describe what the child did.
- Model the activity by acting out a visit you have made. Ask the children to make a story out of it, e.g. "Ms Stevens went to the bus stop. Then she climbed on the bus..."
- Ask the children to do their mimes. Prompt them to think carefully about their journeys. Ask: *What sort of transport did you use? What did you do while you were travelling?*

Cross-curricular link
Geography: observing and expressing views about places and environments

Writing

Objectives To write sentences to match pictures or sequences of pictures (T12); To use experience of stories as a basis for independent writing (T14).

You will need models or pictures of different modes of transport, e.g. bus, car, taxi, plane, ship, helicopter .

- Show the children one model or picture at a time and ask them to write an appropriate sentence, e.g. "We went on a bus."
- Vary the subject, e.g. "Henry went on a ship."

Oxford Reading Tree resources at this level

There is a range of material available at a similar level to these stories which can be used for consolidation or extension.

Stage 1+

Teacher support

- Teacher's Handbook
- Flopover Book
- Big Books for each story in First Sentences
- Guided Reading Cards for First Sentences
- Take-Home Cards for each story
- Extended Stories
- Sequencing Cards Photocopy Masters
- ORT Games Stages 1–3
- Group Activity Sheets Book 1 Stage 1–3
- My Word Book
- Rubber Stamps
- Sequencing Cards Photocopy Masters

Further reading

- Oxford Reading Tree Storybooks for Core Reading
- Fireflies Non-Fiction
- Fact Finder Topic Starters
- Glow-worms Poetry

Electronic

- Clip Art
- Click and Explore and First Talking Stories
- ORT Online www.OxfordReadingTree.com
- Floppy and Friends

For introducing phonics

- First Phonics Stage 1+

For developing phonological awareness

- Alphabet frieze, Tabletop Alphabet Mats, Alphabet Photocopy Masters
- First Story Rhymes, Story Rhymes
- Card Games

OXFORD
UNIVERSITY PRESS

Great Clarendon Street, Oxford OX2 6DP

Oxford University Press is a department of the University of Oxford. It furthers the University's objective of excellence in research, scholarship, and education by publishing worldwide in

Oxford New York

Auckland Bangkok Buenos Aires Cape Town Chennai Dar es Salaam Delhi Hong Kong Istanbul Karachi Kolkata Kuala Lumpur Madrid Melbourne Mexico City Mumbai Nairobi São Paulo Shanghai Taipei Tokyo Toronto

First published 2004

British Library Cataloguing in Publication Data

Data available

Cover illustrations by Joanne Partis

Teacher's Notes: ISBN 0 19 845507 0

10 9 8 7 6 5 4 3 2 1

Page make-up by Fakenham Photosetting, Fakenham, Norfolk

Printed in Great Britain by Ashford Colour Press, Gosport, Hants